Mom, What Do LAWYERS Do?

Roxanne Richards-LeCorps

ISBN: 1482554127
ISBN 13: 9781482554120

For Matthew

Mom, What Do Lawyers Do?

Lawyers study law - rules all people must follow. Lawyers know how to help people do many things, such as buy a house, sell a business, or ask a judge to settle an argument. Adults need attorneys - another word for lawyer - to talk to judges in court and to write things down in a special way that makes them permanent.

Lawyers Settle Arguments Over Accidents

After a car accident, the drivers don't always agree on who was at fault. Lawyers can help to settle the dispute.

Lawyers Help People to Buy or Sell a House

Every time a person buys or sells a home, legal papers must be filed with the government so everyone knows who the owner is. A lawyer reads the contract—the description of the deal between the buyer and the seller—to make sure all the details are correct.

HOUSE FOR SALE
CONTRACT
To:
From:
Subject:
Date:

Lawyers Help People to Get Divorced

If a married couple decides to split up, a lawyer files papers with the court for their divorce. Lawyers also help the couple to make decisions about where the children will live and about money.

Divorce Decree

No.

Plaintiff

versus

Defendant

Decree I[illegible]

reviewed this case

to

order for Alimony

decreed that the

and separated from the

and

support order shall here

economic claims remai

RSELF

claims raised by this action

contracted bet

hereby re

s not yet

bon

the def

for wh

Prothonotary

Deputy

Lawyers Help People to Start or End a Business

Lawyers help businesses run smoothly by making sure all the people involved follow laws. Parents who own their own business may need lawyers to help them correct a lease for a store or go over a contract to buy or sell large amounts of merchandise. The biggest transaction of all could be buying or selling a business.

OPEN
OUT OF BUSINESS

Lawyers Help People to Bring a Lawsuit

A court is a place where a judge listens to both sides of an argument and decides what is fair. When someone thinks another person has done something wrong to them, lawyers help to tell the judge what happened. That is called filing a lawsuit.

LAWSUIT

Lawyers Help People to Plan for the Future

All families need a plan for what will happen if their moms and dads can't work because they have become very sick or disabled. They also need to plan what will happen to their estate—their money, their home, and their belongings—when they die. Those plans make sure children are protected. Lawyers put all those plans in written form called wills and trusts.

WILL

Lawyers Help to Change Laws

Sometimes parents think a law is wrong, or a new law should be made. Lawyers help them write to lawmakers to make those changes.

New Law

Lawyers Help People to Immigrate

Many people were not born in the United States, but they want to live here because they love this country and all the opportunities we have here. Lawyers help immigrants get permission to live here permanently as American citizens.

U.S. CITIZENS

Lawyers Defend People

Sometimes people make mistakes or they are accused of doing something wrong that they did not do. Lawyers help them go to court and tell the judge their side of the story. The judge will decide if the person should be punished, and if so, what he or she has to do to make up for the mistake. It is like when your parents take away your television privileges because you didn't clean your room.

JUDGE

Lawyers Help Parents Adopt Children

Parents can choose to adopt a child. One of the happiest roles a lawyer has is to make that child a permanent member of his or her new family.

Roxanne Richards-LeCorps lives in northern New Jersey. She has hired lawyers to help with real estate and business matters. Her son's questions prompted her to write this book.

Made in the USA
Lexington, KY
09 April 2018